YOU GOT THE POWER

- Have Unshakable Belief i
- Set and Achieve Your Go
- Move beyond Positive Thinking to Positive Doing.
- Win - Keep Trying
- Take Your Business & Career to the Next Level
- Create Your Own Opportunity
- Conquer Fear
- Stop Procrastinating
- Turn Your Adversity into Success
- Associate with Positive People
- Design a Blueprint for Your Life
- Eliminate the Obstacles Blocking Your Path
- Be Successful

You Got The Power!
By
Dayo Olomu

A CIP catalogue record for this title is available from the British Library

Design by: www.byjomedia.com

ISBN 0-9550679-2-8

Published by:

Dayo Olomu *Publishing*

Tel: +44 871 218 1773
Email: info@dayoolomu.com
Website: www.dayoolomu.com

CONTENTS PAGE

Dedication:
To the ordinary people and businesses doing extra-ordinary things.

FOREWARD

Human societies are the results of persistently organized sacrifice and cooperation. The forces that hold us together are a great binding web: though almost abstract, but ever present and unstable. These forces are our mores, morals that pattern existence within a communal living. But when these forces fail, which happens sometimes, we become fragile and perhaps fade into faceless identities. We become prisoners of failure and dependent on fears, afraid to reach our inner circles of life and rise from the distractions of sudden crash. We forget we've got the power.

Dayo Olomu, the oracle of self enhancement, in his new provocative no holds barred book, YOU GOT THE POWER, offers us a determinant out of our life's crises: he enables us, reassures us that it's okay to fear failure, its normal to be interrupted occasionally in life, but it's grossly abnormal to continue being a victim of circumstance.

He encourages us to reach within us, harvest the gift of self-actualization that was blessed us at birth and go forward in our lives. The responsibility to live anew depends on our desire and commitment to sacrifice that includes changing our wardrobe of friends and associates, rebranding our values and daily plans; being able to document our schedules, actions and responsibilities, and against all odds believe in ourselves.

YOU GOT THE POWER is an engaging book. It's a conversation between the author and the reader: You feel an element of self-empowerment from every chapter. The book becomes the reader's mirror to a once thought dead end life that can be resurrected and perfected: a rear view mirror of past mistakes.

I recommend this book to those seeking a redemption to a new life, those in search of a pathway to organized and structured careers and lifestyles because in each of us on earth: We've got the power to be what we want to be.

AZUKA JEBOSE MOLOKWU.
North Carolina, USA

Chapter 1

YOU! YOU!! YOU!!!

This book is one of the most inspirational, powerful and exciting books you will ever read. This dynamic and interesting book will propel you to the next level because "YOU GOT THE POWER!"

If the three most important words in real estate are **location, location, location**; then the three best words that are guaranteed to take you to the top are, YOU! YOU!! YOU!!! . It's all about **YOU**. You must believe in the brand called **YOU**.

A lot of people succeed where others do not believe in them. Rarely does a person succeed when he or she does not believe in himself or herself. That is why you must believe in yourself. You've got to have self-belief in order to achieve anything in life.

In my earthly journeys, I've encountered tough times. And through the journeys of my intriguing life, I had faced adversities that challenged my desire to continue. But I never gave up. My dear reader, I am an example of how anyone could overcome adversity and succeed, thus becoming an inspiration to others.

I arrived in London in the cold winter of January 1996, full of hope and expectations. I suspected that life in the United Kingdom would be a roller coaster. I hoped that by being a British citizen, the challenges would be to my advantage. However, I was shocked to discover that I was immediately a victim of identity theft: a crook had stolen my birth certificate, used it to collect my national insurance card, applied and received a credit card and opened a bank account. I also found out that I was married! The only thing left was that the crook forgot to invite me to the wedding! Everywhere I went, I was told somebody was using my name: the authorities didn't know who the real Dayo Olomu was.

The sad experience with my identity being stolen almost discouraged me from settling into a new life in, United Kingdom, my birthplace. I was ready to quit and return to Nigeria. I was at an emotional crossroads; the depth of which I never knew existed. If I had no belief in myself, I would have gone back to Nigeria less than six months after arriving in London.

Most people fail not because they lack the skills or talent to reach their goals, but because they don't believe they can reach these goals. Believing in yourself is also necessary when you face scepticism from family and friends. Self-belief will carry you through, allowing you to continue with your life's goal irrespective of any negativity you may face.

I was almost discouraged from writing my first book, "4 Indispensable Strategies for Success." The first person I told about my desire to write that book said, "Dayo, you must be a joker and a dreamer! What do you know?" But I believed in myself, my commitment and ability to write and publish the book. Because of these qualities, I was able to achieve my set goals and the book became a best seller in the UK and Nigeria. When no one believed in me, I believed in myself and achieved more than anyone ever thought possible.

Venus Williams, the Olympic gold medallist and professional tennis champion expressed it best thus: "You have to believe in yourself when nobody else does. That's what makes you a winner".

The Law of Belief states that, "Whatever you believe, with emotion, becomes your reality. Example, if you absolutely believe that you are destined to be a great success in your field, and you walk, talk, act and behave exactly the same way a successful person would, then you will eventually develop the mind-set of a high performer. And as you develop the mind-set, you will begin to get the results that match. Your beliefs will become actual facts, they will become tangible. Your beliefs will become your reality.

Chapter 2

FEAR FACTOR

Have you ever asked yourself what keeps you from reaching your full potential or from doing what you are capable of? For many of us, it is fear. The biggest barrier that we have to overcome is fear; fear of rejection, fear of ridicule, fear of making decisions, fear of change, fear of confrontation, fear of loss, fear of success and certainly – fear of failure! It is this fear, and all its associations – like worry, anxiety, and self-doubt, that paralyze you and keep you from succeeding.

"FEAR is an ancient topic in the history of human race. It's enough to make you sick. It causes some people a constant and gnawing pain in the pit of the stomach. Others drink more or smoke more because of fear. Fear killed dreams and ruined careers than all other causes combined. The number one killer of our dreams at work and at home, is fear. The longer I live, the more I realize that FEAR is the worst enemy of the human species. And it's been with us. The Book of Genesis speaks of fear and it appears throughout the Bible, Torah and Koran. We should not forget the classic line from the Old Testament delivered by Job: "That which I feared most has come upon me."

Stop and think about it. Most children are fearless creatures (unless an adult has already instilled a lot of fear in them). Teenagers and even young adults continue to display mostly courageous attitudes. But as we age, we grow more fearful. Perhaps we realize there is a lot at stake. Any mistake could be life changing. But rather, we should definitely become more fearless with age because wisdom (which usually comes with age) makes us more apt to see the truth in a situation. That fear is a myth, a creation of a weak mind, is illustrated by this acronym: FEAR- False Evidence Appearing Real.

I experience fear of poverty when I was growing up in Nigeria. I was born in Islington, North London, and taken to Nigeria when I was two years old. I had an early jolt in life. My father died when I was just eight years old. My father's death changed my family. He was the provider and head of our household. His sudden death fragmented the early years care, love and protection from a dear dad and husband. Life became a struggle. My mother, a widow, sold virtually all her personal belongings to send me to school and raise me. I greatly benefited from her wealth of wisdom. I learnt from her great moral and spiritual values along with the virtues of hard work. She made me believe that the keys to success are hard work, faith in God, absolute belief and self-actualisation and realisation.

I celebrated my 10th birthday at a public transport bus garage and parking lot in Lagos, hawking cold drinks and biscuits to support my mother. The best thing that happened to me was growing up without the privilege of wealthy parents. I hustled for anything and everything that I wanted. Those experiences were far from a drawback, in fact, they were definite advantages for me. Hence, when I left secondary school, I decided to make my life a miracle, a decision to succeed against all odds. That decision has been my driving force; I backed it with action and conquered the fear of poverty.

Today that little boy who celebrated his 10th birthday at a bus garage in Lagos selling cold drinks, biscuits and whose identity was stolen when he came back to live in London, is an Inspirational Speaker; Human Resources & Business Transformation Consultant, Executive/Business Coach;; Success & Winning Strategist; Best Selling Author; Award winning Master of Ceremonies; An agent of positive change; TV Personality and best of everything, a loving husband and wonderful father.

I had friends who were once seemingly fearless super-achievers. However, having reached middle age, they fell for fear, became afraid of life and living: Their fear syndrome affected their qualities of life significantly. They have surrendered their dreams and their lives to fear: Fear of failure, Fear of rejection, fear of change, fear of success, and fear of making decisions, fear of responsibility, and fear of commitment. It is fear (and all of its agents, such as worry, anxiety, depression, and self-doubt) that will turn your dream of success into a chilling nightmare: a trauma that may lead you into depression.

People, often say to me at speaking engagements, “I can't afford to pursue my dream because I don't have enough money." I asked them how much they needed. Usually the answers were, "I don't know. But I know I don't have enough:" Same thing with time. Are you complaining that you don't have the time to pursue your dreams or that you are busy, while never actually scheduling an hour to see how you might break your dream into smaller projects? Jim Rohn, America's foremost business philosopher reasoned: "Don't mistake movement for achievement. It's easy to get faked out by being busy. The question is: busy doing what?"

Vic Johnson, founder of AsAManThinketh.net approached the fear syndrome thus: “Fear can be defeated because fear is a learned response in the first place. It’s said that we were only born with two fears: the fear of falling and the fear of loud noises. Every other fear you have was learned!” One thing you must never allow fear to do is stop you from achieving your dreams. Never stop until all your dreams come true. Remember, obstacles and fear are the things you see when your eyes are taken off the desired target.

One thing you must never allow fear to do is to stop you from realizing your dreams. Never stop until all your dreams come true.

Action Cures Fear

To conquer the fear of public speaking I joined Toastmasters International. It was in the summer of 2003 when I walked into a pub in Croydon. It was the meeting of the Toastmasters Club. When I saw how the people spoke so eloquently there, I asked myself: when will I be able to do this? It took me three months to achieve my first engagement as a speaker. But I did it at last and I am still doing it. Today I am not only an advanced toastmaster but I am also a competent leader and the charter president of a toastmasters' club.

I spent my birthday of 2006 with Tony Robbins attending his "Unleash the Power". *Fire walking* is the act of walking barefoot over a bed of hot embers or stones. The Fire walk is the dramatic highlight of Unleash the Power Within, the introductory three-day seminar given by personal development guru Tony Robbins. It was designed to be both a challenge to the participants, a symbol of the change they can make to their lives and it also served as a very effective marketing tool for Robbins' pricey products and seminars.

This is where sane humans prance across several yards of smoking-hot, burning coals while their fellow higher achievers and some tribal drummers chant on. And most don't burn their feet, including me.

During a fire-walking event, you almost always see a large, glowing bed of burning coals. The bed may be 10 feet long or so. And the glowing coals are real. People actually do walk across the red-hot coals in bare feet.

I remember the first time I did bar bending in 2007. I was introduced to this, by Tosin Ogunnusi, UK's leading Empowerment coach. Tosin and I stood six feet apart, rested each end of a six-foot long iron bar in the soft spot located in the front of our throats, just under our Adams's apple. We looked into each other's eyes and concentrated on both our current power, as well as having drawn up former powerful images of us by the instructor. We uttered the: Yes, Yes, Yes, I was ready: on the count three, we began to walk toward each other. UNBELIEVABLE! Yes, right in front of our eyes and throats, that six-foot long once staff iron bar bent into a U shape between us, the belly of the U iron bar touching the ground. What a glorious and exciting illustration that our minds have incredible powers, if only we can channel them. My message to those who fear is that you can do something. Take action, feel fear and do it anyway.

Dr. Thomas J. Stanley, author of the best seller *The Millionaire Next Door*, surveyed nearly 1,000 US millionaires in his book *The Millionaire Mind*, and what he found may surprise you.

The two characteristics that self-made millionaires had in common are: "think differently from the crowd, and they have a strong belief in themselves." Surprisingly when I met Sir Richard Branson of Virgin Atlantic, Robin Seiger of Robin Seiger International, Prof Pat Utomi of Lagos Business School, & Barry Gibbon - the man who turned Burger King around, I asked them the secret to their success and they all said, "You must believe in yourself".

If you want to be successful at anything, believing in yourself is the most important thing that can help you get there. When I was growing up in Lagos I used to think that success was reserved for those who were born into wealthy families, with good university degrees, and to whom every advantage had been given. Later in life I realised that no matter what life throws at you, you could be successful. There are people who have succeeded beyond all expectations, regardless of race or colour. Humans can turn nothing into something, pennies into a fortune and disaster into success. You too have the power to turn your sorrows to joy.

My role models are common people doing uncommon and extraordinary things because they often, sowed the seeds of businesses and entrepreneurial revolutions we see today, time after time. They dared to be different because they took the roads less travelled. They are my inspiration and they energise me. They are not just an inspiration to me, but to everyone. They believed they could do it and they often did. If you believe that you are less than someone, because of lack of education, looks, talent, background or ability, take courage from their achievements and go for it! More than 75% of self-made millionaires in Britain and America began with nothing or in many cases, less than nothing. If they can do it you can too! Believing in you is more important than knowledge, training or schooling; statistics tell us that 205 of America's millionaires never set foot in a college and 21 of the 222 American's listed as billionaires in 2003, never received their diploma. Although education and a commitment to lifelong learning are essential to success, a formal degree isn't a requirement. Jim Rohn said that standard education will get you jobs, but self-education will make you a fortune.

Create Your Opportunity

Don't wait for the right opportunity to fall into your lap; if you do, then you will be waiting a long time because it never will.

According to George Bernard Shaw "The people who get on in this world are people who get up and look for the circumstances they want, and if they can't find them, they make them."

Create your own opportunities and make things happen. You have the ability to choose. All you need to carve your own path is the confidence and the belief that you can succeed at anything you set out to do, no matter what the odds are. Don't wait for someone else to give you an opportunity to prove yourself. Stop depending on others to create favourable circumstances or offer you handouts.

You can change anything for yourself that you wish to change. I challenge you to do that because you can change. If you don't like how something is panning out for you; change it. If something isn't enough; change it. If something doesn't suit you; change it. If something doesn't please you; change it. You don't ever have to be the same after today.

Stephen Covey, in his book: *The 8th Habit* said: "Next to life itself, the power to choose is your greatest gift. Fundamentally, we are a product of choice, not nature (genes) or nurture (upbringing, environment). Certainly genes and cultures often influence very powerfully, but they do not determine. The essence of being human is being able to direct your own life."

Chapter 3
SET GOALS

Do you set goals? If you don't have any set goals. I urge you to begin the process and set goals. Recent research, sponsored by UK Visa, revealed that 23% of British men and women admit to having never set themselves a goal. In a nutshell they live goalless lives.

Some British people may show low levels of ambition but the research highlights that Britons who set themselves target do achieve their goals. Only one per cent of those surveyed in the UK said that they never reach their goals with over half (57%) saying that they 'usually' achieve their targets. The research highlights that when you set goals, you often achieve them. Goals are dreams with deadlines. David J. Schwartz, in his book *The Magic of Thinking Big* described a goal as "an objective, a purpose."

A goal is more than a dream; it is a dream being acted upon. Nothing happens; no forward steps are taken until a goal is established. Without goals, individuals merely wander through life. They stumble along, never knowing where they are going, and consequently they never get anywhere. Goals are as essential to success as air is to life. No one ever stumbles into success without a goal; no one ever lives without air. Get a clear picture of where you want to go. Imagine a life without a goal to accomplish. I am always amazed at many people I see every day who just live aimlessly without a goal. They live, not knowing that a life without a goal is a life spread so wide and yet so thin. It is like going on a journey without a destination. Their consolation is: "what will be, will be." These people live by what I call, the Laws of Accident: "there is no way we can control what happens to us and everything just happens by accident."

Unfortunately, whether or not we realize it, a vast majority of men and women live their lives by this law. They have no goal beyond the short term, they make no plans, they don't really feel they are in control of their own destinies and they just hope that somehow things will work out. Brain Tracy calls this "blind optimism" – the most wilfully ignorant is one that imagines an unemployed person will get a high-flying job without having the prerequisite skills. Are you one of them? If the answer is yes, then wake up and face reality. The moment you set a goal, a light goes on in your future. When we set goals, we develop directions, we become focused, we channel our energy and we ultimately accomplish more in a short time than we could accomplish in years.

To create a balanced life, your goals must cover the following eight areas:
1. Spiritual
2. Family
3. Health
4. Career or Business
5. Wealth/Finance
6. Self-development
7. Personal Needs
8. Contribution to society or Legacy

A few years ago, one of my mentors gave me a copy of Earl Nightingale's audiocassette program called *The Strangest Secret*. In it he said that the reason why people with goals succeed in life, and people without them fail is because of these six words, "We become what we think about." He continued, "A person who is thinking about a concrete and worthwhile goal is going to reach it, because that's what he's thinking about. The person who has no goal, who doesn't know where he's going and whose thoughts must therefore be thoughts of confusion, anxiety, fear and worry – his life becomes one of frustration, fear, anxiety and worry. And if he thinks about nothing … he becomes nothing." To Earl Nightingale, "that is the key to success and the key to failure".

Write it Down
When you set goals, write your goals down on paper and in detail. Always think on paper. A goal that is not in writing is not a goal. It is merely a wish; thus it has no energy behind it. According to Brain Tracy, one of my teachers, "People with clear, written goals, accomplish far more in a shorter period of time than people without them could ever imagine."

The turning point of my life happened on my 35th in birthday in 2000 when I went on a pilgrimage to Jerusalem. I sat down and wrote 40 goals that I hoped to achieve by the time I turned 40. Some of them included having six professions that would generate multiple streams of income. The professions were to become a business strategist, trainer, journalist, motivational speaker, life coach and an author. I also wrote that I would publish a magazine; speak to audiences in the United States, United Kingdom and Nigeria. The goals also included becoming an entrepreneur, have my own website, meeting Sir Richard Branson and America's Inspirational speaker, Les Brown. By my 39th birthday I had achieved everything, except writing a book; I achieved that on my 40th birthday. At the time I wrote down the goals in Jerusalem, I was a postman studying for a degree in Business Information Systems at the University of East London. I was able to achieve the goals I had set because I believed in myself and took action. To achieve your goals write them on a small sheet of paper (or your smart phone) and break them into manageable parts. I write my goals on a small sheet of paper and put the paper in my wallet. I encourage you to do the same. I look at it twice daily. Successful people have their eyes focused on a goal and that provides energy. The point is this: energy increases and multiplies when you set a desired goal and resolve to work towards it.

I used this same principle, of writing goals on paper and breaking them down. To set a goal to run the London Marathon, I started by running the 10 kilometres. After that I participated in the Fleet Half Marathon before I completed the Flora London Marathon with a smile on my face.

About three per cent of adults write their goals and plans that they work on every day. When you sit down and write out your goals, you reposition yourself into the top three per cent of people in society, and you will soon start to get the same results as they did. The act of writing your goals down tremendously increases your chance of success. Write them down! Then, keep your notes where you can see and read them every day.

Whatever your goals are, ensure that you plan them thoroughly. Every goal must take the form of a plan. The old saying that you "get what you plan for" is true. Your dreams won't just happen. You need to sit down, on a regular basis, and plan out your strategy for achieving your dreams. Think through all of the details. Break the whole plan down into small, workable parts. Then set a time frame for accomplishing each task on your "master plan', and take a step, each day, towards achieving them. That is the key to peak performance and maximum achievement. Successful people get where they want to go by following a strategic plan. They learn what it takes to get ahead. We know that to build a house, it takes a plan – a blueprint, but we sometimes forget that to build a successful life, also requires a blueprint.

Visualize Your Goals

Once you have written down all your goals, the next step on your journey to the top is to activate the creative power of your subconscious mind and visualize your goals. I learnt this process from Jack Canfield, famous for *Chicken Soup for the Soul*. "The process of visualization is really quite simple. If one of your objectives is to own a jaguar, then close your eyes and picture yourself driving the model and colour of jaguar you desired. Make the image as clear, vivid and bright as possible". Jack Canfield said.

This applies to any goal you make – whether it's in the area of work, play, family, personal finances, relationships or community. Write down each of your goals and objectives, then review them, affirm them and visualize them every day.

When you awake, each morning and before you go to bed each night, read through your list of goals, pausing after each one to recreate a mental visual image of what the accomplished goal would look like. Continue through the list until you have visualized each goal as complete and fulfilled. The whole process will take between 5-10 minutes, depending on how many goals you have. If you pray or meditate, do your visualization right after. The deepened state you achieve through meditation or prayer will heighten the impact of your visualization. I believe the first step towards a successful goal achievement, regardless of your process or steps you follow in setting your goals, is to absolutely believe that you will accomplish your aims.

David Schwartz wrote in *The Magic of Thinking Big*, "Believe Big. The size of your success is determined by the size of your belief. Think little goals and expect little achievements. Think big goals and win big success. Remember this too - big ideas and big plans are often easier - certainly no more difficult than small ideas and small plans."

Chapter 4

ACTION

The secret to your dream and success doesn't lie in the specifics; it lies in your willingness to start. Take ACTION TODAY! ACTION is the great divider. It separates the doers from the dreamers and the walkers from the talkers.

I am for action. People who are successful always take action. Anyone who has ever been successful has done something.

Think about it! Even someone who is a successful 'thinker' (as opposed to a 'doer') is usually known because he did something that tells us about his or her success. Sir Richard Branson founded Virgin Atlantic; Tony Ryan founded Ryan air; Levis Strauss invented jeans; Alexander Graham Bell invented the telephone; Dr John S. Pemberton invented Coca-Cola; Willis Carrier brought us the comfort zone with air conditioning; The Wright Brothers built the world's first aeroplane; Richie Dayo Johnson founded Richmond Johnson Academy, Stephen Covey wrote "The Seven Habits of Highly Effective People" and "The 8th Habit: From Effectiveness to Greatness", Thomas Edison invented the electric light bulb, Mark Elliot Zuckerberg co-founded Facebook, Dame Anita Roddick founded Body Shop, Mary Kay Ash founded Mary Kay Cosmetics Steve Jobs co-founded Apple, Lee Byung-chul founded Samsung. The list is endless. What they all have in common is ACTION.

They did something, and they did it with conviction! They took action and that is the reason we talk, read about and celebrate them today.

Once they developed a plan, they simply started. They acted. Create your own opportunities and forge your own future.

Self-belief and the courage to see it through is what will carry you from a life of mediocrity and under-achievement; into a world where you can be the winner you aspire to be. When you have something to do, don't put it off, do it right away. Stop procrastinating. Why do we procrastinate? The reason is bad planning and lack of time. For many people it is because they are striving for perfection. One of my senior colleagues, Richie Dayo Johnson, often says, "An ineffective plan executed today is better than a perfect plan delayed till next year." It is better to try and fail than fail to try. One proverb captures it thus: 'After all is said and done; more is usually said than done.' The person determined to achieve maximum success understands the principle that progress is made one step at a time. A house is built one brick at a time. Every big accomplishment is a series of little accomplishments stringed together. The journey of a thousand mile begins with a single step. However, completing a journey of a thousand mile requires that you keep walking!

Take Action Everyday

- Do something every day.
- Have a goal for the day.
- Start Small.
- A simple plan will, more likely, bear fruit than something elaborate. Remember, in transforming your life, the value of small things consistently practiced over time.
- Starbucks built a global brand one cup at a time. What started, as a single store on Seattle's waterfront has grown into a company with over 1,600 stores worldwide, with a new one opening every working business day.
- Do not be not afraid of going slowly; only be only afraid of standing still – Chinese proverb
- Every minute matters in one's life. If you don't know, there are only 527, 040 minutes in a leap year – utilize them wisely!

Chapter 5
WHO DO YOU HANG OUT WITH?

Dr David McClelland of Harvard University spent twenty five years researching success and achievement and his conclusion was this: your reference groups, the people with whom you associate on a regular basis, largely determine your success or failure in life. His conclusion was that the people you associate with on a daily basis would determine 90% of everything that happens to you in life. You begin to think; walk, act, dress and talk like them, and you tend to hold the same opinions of the people you are around most. So associating with like-minded people is vital to making successful changes. In the article, Dr McClelland suggested that one should select their associations with care.

In selecting your association, the people you want to be hanging out with should be people who are going where you are heading. People who add value to your life. They are a "Network of Enablers". In case you do not have these people in your life, start thinking of how you can attract them today. One of the best ways to attract them is by embracing the concept of professional networking. In his book titled *Personal Networking: How to Make Your Connections Count*, Mike Cope described professional networking as "a set of close contact or associates who will help deliver your value to the market. The key thing is that these are people who will help you in the market. "

Michael Masterson in his book, The *Reluctant Entrepreneur* described them as "Power Network". "Your power network is comprised of all the people you know who can make a positive difference in your future. They include your mentors, consultants, competitors, vendors, colleagues, and people in high places who have resources and connections you lack." He said.

After meeting your enablers, nurture and build the relationship with them so that you can leverage it later for either your career advancement or business success. In a report titled "Developing Business Leaders for 2010," which appeared in The Conference Board, it said that "one *of the four key essential leadership skills is relationship building/network building"*.

An article in MIT Sloan management review "The Social Side of Performance says: "What really distinguishes high performers from the rest of the pack is their ability to maintain and leverage personal networks. The most effective, create and tap large, diversified networks that are rich in experience and span all organizational boundaries.

Renowned author Harvey Mackay says, "If I had to name the single characteristic shared by all truly successful individuals, I'd say it's the ability to create and nurture a network of contacts."

I became a strategic networker and started professionally in 2003 where things were not going the way I wanted in my business. I undertook a network analysis by listing out all the names in my telephone contact and started categorizing them. I created five categories namely

- Stressors
- Family
- Friends
- Enablers
- Mentors

Surprisingly a lot of people fall into the Stressors category and only have five people in the enabler's category and one person in the mentor's category. To be successful in life and career you need more enablers and mentors and that is what I have been able to achieve today which have impacted my life and bank balance positively.

There is this proverb in Africa that says 'show me your friend and I will tell you who you are.' Bob Proctor, one of my teachers once told me that: "The people you associate with will either make or break you".

Your network is a great source of leverage. When you need something you don't have, you reach out to your network to see if someone has it.

Almost all successful individuals understand the power of leverage. Using leverage accelerates success in any endeavour. You may become successful without using leverage but, if you aren't using it that means you are willing to compromise the level of success, speed, and time necessary to get to each level.

I continually leverage my contacts to accomplish what others may say is impossible. And, in using that leverage, I make sure that it is always beneficial for both sides of the equation. In a nutshell, develop your social capital and build a network of enablers.

Chapter 6

HOW DO YOU START YOUR DAY?

Do you just wake up in the morning, have your bath and go to work? If you answered yes: then that is not how to start an eventful day.

Spend time each day to think about your future, your life, your values and your choices. Decide where you are going and write it down. I do it early in the morning; some of my clients perform this exercise before they go to bed at night. Find what works out best for you and do it.

My daily activities begin every morning with devotion service alongside my family, then a treadmill exercise to help me with my fitness mentally, intellectually spiritually and emotionally. These activities which include Bible sessions with my family and push-ups exercise are done in the golden hours of our mornings.

During this process I look at my list of things to do for the day, and assign the ABCD strategy. A means Action Now, B means before the end of the day, C means it can't wait till tomorrow and D means delegate or delete it.

Music, like other art forms, appeal to the conscious and subconscious mind. Once music is in the subconscious, its melody and lyrics can influence and motivate you. The regular playing of the song will help you recall the lyrics and eventually, your subconscious state will imbibe the possible 'meanings' that the song implies.

Our family listen and dance to music together as part of our daily morning devotions. Good Music helps to energise you for the day and build a perfect mind set.

Since music can greatly influence a person emotionally and mentally, it can be used as a good exercise on how to build a perfect mind set. Music could rub to a person's conscious and subconscious. Try it and it will leave you with an all-day smile.

It is important you go to bed early to get a good night's sleep. Benjamin Franklin noted that: "early to bed, early to rise makes a man (or woman) healthy and wise." Keeping an ambitious rigorous daily schedule seems to help. If you do what you've always done, you will get what you've always gotten. I guarantee it!

Peak performance people know the value of controlling their daily directions. They know that starting the day with some inspiration reading or vibrant music or stimulating conversation will tend to invigorate the entire day. That is why every motivational speaker recommends listening to tapes in the morning, rather than the bad news on TV.

Imagine what could happen to your life if you did this every morning. Keeping an ambitious, rigorous daily schedule seems to help. If you do what you've always done, you will get what you've always got. I guarantee it!

My life has been the quintessential tale of struggling and overcoming adversity in the UK and Nigeria in order to reach self-actualization. If I can do it, anybody can do it.

After one of my training sessions at the University of Greenwich I met a woman, a mother of eight children, who was pursuing a degree in law. That shows you the power of self-belief and self-determination. My core belief is that, within YOU lies the power to change your life and make your dreams come true. Intensely believe that you can succeed! Believe that you can become successful! Strongly believe that you can get whatever you want - many times over! Believe it is possible to solve your problems. Tremendous things happen to a believer. So believe the answer will come, and it will.

Napoleon Hill wrote: "You can be anything you want to be, if only you believe with sufficient conviction and act in accordance with your faith, for whatever the mind can conceive and believe, the mind can achieve." I want you to believe in yourself and start thinking that you have what it takes to become who you really want to be. You've got to start thinking of yourself in the future and see yourself there. Do something every single day that moves you in the direction of your current primary goal. Develop the discipline of doing something 365 days each day of the year, every year that moves you forward. You will be absolutely astonished at how much you can accomplish when you daily utilise this formula in your life. I have learnt that successful people all have a strong desire to succeed. They then back their decision to succeed with action. Successful people have a consummate belief in themselves, when disappointments occur, they press on. They choose to search for solutions rather than give up and quit.

Make a Decision TODAY to set goals and write your plans on paper. It is crucial that you take action immediately. To be successful, you have to do what successful people do, and successful people are highly action-oriented. Remember people don't get to heaven without dying. As the famous Nike sports strapline says: "Just do it!"

Chapter 7

BE EXTRA-ORDINARY

One of the things that I have learnt from successful people is their strong desire to succeed. They back their desires with actions. Successful people have absolute belief in themselves and when setbacks or tragedies occur, they do not give up; instead they see these adversaries as opportunities for growth because success thrives on adversity. What separate ordinary people from extraordinary people are the little extra things. When you make a decision to go the extra mile and take action and believe in yourself you will become extraordinary and that is who you are.

Here are the quotes from three great men I admire:

America's foremost business philosopher, Jim Rohn, once said, "The big challenge is to become all that you have the possibility of becoming. You cannot believe what it does to the human spirit to maximize your potential and stretch yourself to the limit." In the words of Norman Vincent Peale, "People become really quite remarkable when they start thinking that they can do things, when they believe in themselves they have the first secret of success."

Finally, Henry Ford, an auto industry billionaire, whose formal education was limited and is rumoured to have lasted about three years, began his business career under the handicap of poverty, illitcracy and ignorance. He said, "One of the greatest discoveries a man makes, one of his greatest surprises is to find he can do what he was afraid he couldn't do." He also said that "if you believe you can or you believe you can't you'll be right."

You are a unique person. You have an unusual gift and untapped potential. You have a unique history. You have a unique temperament and experience. You have a unique footprint and voiceprint. You have magnificent talents, capabilities and skills. You have an extraordinary DNA. Some have even suggested that your DNA carries with it the wisdom of previous generations. You have a unique genetic code. You have a unique destiny that only you can fulfil. Above all you are endowed with the seeds of greatness.

YOU GOT THE POWER!

About the Author

Dayo Olomu, As An Agent of Positive Change

Dayo Olomu is a leading human capital development and business transformation strategist, based in London, United Kingdom. He is an accomplished inspirational speaker and award winning event host. He is also the bestselling author of "4 Indispensable Strategies for Success" and audio programme, "You Got The Power" which was sent to more than 180 countries by Success University (now known as World Ventures) in September 2008. He is the vice chairman of Chartered Institute of Personnel Development (CIPD) South London; Founding President of Croydon Communicators Toastmasters; Member, Governing Council, Davidson Primary School in Croydon, Surrey; Founder, African Professional Speakers Academy and President, Nigerian Trainers & Speakers Consortium (NTSC) UK.

Dayo Olomu is highly sought-after for being uniquely engaging and profoundly outstanding. He is articulate and irrepressible, addressing and training more than 100,000 people each year on personal and professional development, achieving peak performance, wealth creation, success, motivation, networking, mentoring, management, relationship, personal success, customer service and goal setting. His audience also benefits from his lectures on leadership, good governance, business growth, relationship building, strategic positioning, decision-making, workflow management and many other diverse topics.

Renowned for his passion, high-energy and inspirational presentation, Dayo Olomu's compelling style is a unique fusion of Nigerian and British culture, which gives his presentations a distinctive, oratory edge and enables him to get his powerful messages across to audiences with warmth, passion, energy and substance.

He travels all over Europe, North America, Africa and United Arab Emirates impacting positively on professionals and businesses, and encouraging them to achieve extraordinary results, increase performance and profit exponentially.

His passion for adding value to lives, growing people and businesses gets him out of bed early every morning. His experience of interacting with people for over two decades has led him to discovering that if we help people to see themselves as they can, not as they are; then the way they think, the way they feel and the way they act will eventually be altered, thereby resulting in achieving optimum performance.

Listed in the first edition of UK's Who's Who of Black Achievers (published in 1999/2000), Dayo Olomu won the exemplary Nigerian Award for hard work and integrity in 2004 and also bagged the Competent Toastmaster Award from Toastmasters International in the same year.

In 2006, he received the Advance Toastmaster Bronze and Competent Leader Awards from Toastmasters International and was consequently named as one of the five most popular Black Speakers in the UK in June 2007.

He bagged the Advance Communicator Silver Award from Toastmasters International in 2008 and he was also bestowed with the Nigeria's Ambassador of Hope in the Diaspora Award in the following year.

In 2010 he won the Male Personality of the Year in UK at Life Changers Award and in 2011, he won the Leadership Award category at the Gathering of Africa's Best Awards. In 2012 was honoured with the prestigious BEFFTA (Black Entertainment Film, Fashion and Arts) Awards. In 2014, he was honoured with the Ambassador of Personal Development in UK Award by Marketing Ministers UK.

Dayo Olomu has also turned his worthy selfless service of enhancing professional lives into that of a philanthropist; donating his time and career in service to less privileged society. An admirer of give back attitude, Olomu in recognition of human responsibilities, interconnection and interrelations, volunteered and completed the Flora London Marathon to raise money and create awareness for Leukaemia in 2007 and in April 2008 he completed the Flora London Marathon again to create awareness and raise funds for Hearts of Gold Children's Hospices-the first children's hospice and respite care facility in Nigeria.

He currently supports three charities namely: Focus on Disability Foundation, a UK registered charity that provides mobility aids to the physically challenged people and Croydon Nightwatch, has empowered and assisted thousands of homeless vulnerable people to turn around their lives, from being homeless and unemployed to re-settling and providing them with a stable, enriched life.

In March 2010, he completed the Fleet Half Marathon to create awareness and raise funds for 'Wish for Africa' and in August 2011, he skydived to create awareness and raise funds for the Desmond Tutu Foundation. He also completed the Croydon Half Marathon in 2013 to raise funds for the homeless people in Croydon.

During his spare time he volunteers as a career development coach with Careers Development Group where he provides coaching on interview skills, goal setting, self development, confidence and motivation building to those seeking employment. He is a Business Mentor with Start up Loan, where he mentors those who are starting out in business. He is also a Key Person of Influence in the Diaspora community and has been involved in the successful delivery of key projects like Nigerian Centenary Awards (2014), Nigerian Olympic Community (2012) and Nigeria at 50 Celebrations (2010).

Dayo Olomu holds an honours degree in Business Information Systems, a Diploma in Coaching, a Post Graduate Certificate in Further Education, a Master's degree in Human Resources and an honorary doctorate in leadership and communications. He is a Chartered Member of Chartered Institute of Personnel and Development (CIPD).

He lives in Croydon, Surrey, with his wife Sade (who he fondly called, Goddess) and children. He enjoys running the marathon, skydiving, and mountain climbing; fire walking, forest walking, board breaking, bar bending and most importantly making a difference. His long-term goal is to space travel, as he believes "Nothing will compare to seeing the earth from space".

TESTIMONIALS/ACCOLADES

Dayo Olomu speaks to all but speaks to one. His valuable insight resonates with you personally even in the midst of several other people in the same seminar. Highly recommended. – Shola Ajani, CEO, Human Capital Asset Management Group

---

Thank you for your presentation on Networking for the CIPD HR Ambitions 111 to enable our members in developing their networking skills. You engaged people to start actively making professionals relationships, which happened during the day. You showed participants how to developing and maintain those relationships in ways they understood and showed them how to maximise those relationships. - Brenda English MBA, Council Representative, CIPD South London Branch

---

Going through your profile and activities give me great joy! You are a source of inspiration for a whole generation! More grease! Chief Segun Odegbami

---

International Centre for Development Initiatives (ICDI) United Kingdom and our Nigeria partners, Leading Edge Academy (LEA) want to say a BIG THANK YOU to you, and express our sincere and heartfelt appreciation for the unflinching support you accorded us, for your amazing presentation and for sharing your talent and expertise with our conference delegates during the one week event in London. - Olalekan Fadeyi, Programs & Policy Director

---

"I enjoyed your talk on Networking. Very inspiring – Mr Odein Ajumogobia SAN – Nigeria's Former Minister of Foreign Affairs".

"Thanks for your presentation on 'Networking'. I was blown-over by the whole pitch on the importance of networking. The whole session from beginning to the end was excellent and opened my mind to the 'open' door that awaits you when you network. - Vivian Heckman, HR Practitioner"

Dayo took part as a speaker for the event Les Brown's London UK tour at Central Hall Westminster. Dayo did a fantastic opening, his delivery as a speaker was on a level that was recognised sharing the stage with Les Brown. I received great reviews about Dayo from Les Brown and the Platinum Speakers from the US who were also at the event speaking. That is why Dayo demands the respect of all his titles, too much to mention, but as a speaker and a motivator he certainly gets my vote hands down for one of the UK's top inspirational speakers - Herald Bradnock, CEO, Reishore Marketing UK

Dayo did not only unknot the knotty aspect of networking at our event, but he also took our attendees through the very engaging process of practical networking. We wish him greater attainment in many ways. Lekan Fatodu, Publisher, Checkout Magazine, UK

Dayo touched everyone present in the room, even the accomplished, the confident and the self-assured. We were truly inspired by his story and his delivery was down to earth, light and yet powerful. On the back of his delivery a new light has been ignited in the lives of individuals who had otherwise given up. – Demola Adesina, CEO, Testing Academy, London

---

Thank you for your valued contribution to the Black History Month event at the Clocktower complex. The audience appreciated your talk and many comments forms were filled in with encouraging words and compliments from the audience. - Krishna Ray, Ethnic Minorities Information Officer, Croydon Council, Croydon Clocktower, Katharine Street, Croydon, CR9 1ET

This is to specially thank you for making Turning Point Seminar a success. Thank you for your life-changing presentations, which will go a long way in the history of our dear nation, Nigeria. - S.A. Paul, CEO Liberty Communications, Port Harcourt Nigeria

---

I want to thank you for agreeing, at such notice to give a brief inspirational talk to our staff. They were inspired by it and I am particularly appreciative. - T.A. Ejueyitchie, MD Premier Records

Dayo Olomu's Services & Programmes

Services:

• Consultancy - PR, Branding, Social Media, Career & Organisation Development
• Design and lead workshops, trainings and seminars - on Leadership, Good Governance, Business Growth, Wealth Creation, Success, Motivation, Branding, Career and Personal Development
• Coaching – peak performance, executive and business transformation coaching by telephone, face to face, email and social media.
• Facilitation – expert in facilitating groups of all sizes from team meetings to chairing large conferences.
• Master of Ceremonies (MC) – for AGM's, seminars, workshops, conferences, meetings, product launches, press conferences, birthday parties, weddings, banquets and balls, corporate events Civic Events and Receptions, charity/gala balls and auctions, award ceremonies, anniversaries, official openings and corporate dinners

Contact Dayo Olomu for any of the following programmes:
• Dayo Olomu's Hold-Your-Hand-At-Every-Step Gold Mentoring Program
• One-one-One High Level Consulting With Dayo Olomu
• How to Fast Track Your Career & Get Your Next Job
• Invent Your World & Make It Happen
• Power Up Your Presentations Skills & Earn Addition Money as a Speaker

• How to Start & Run a Successful Business Without Quitting Your Day Job
• Strategic Positioning
• Multiple Streams of Income Executive Coaching

Keynote Presentations by Dayo Olomu
1. A Motivational Speech Based on Dayo Olomu's Life Story
2. Strategic Positioning: Be the Light & Salt of the Business World
3. Leadership of the 21st Century: Extraordinary Times Demand Extraordinary Leadership
4. How to Make Social Media Stand Up and Dance for You (Tips, Tricks and Insights into How Social Media Can Be Exploited to Grow a Business or Career)
5. Customer Experience Management - From Leads to Raving Customers
9. Passions to Profits: How to Develop Multiple Streams of Income
10. You Got the Power
12. Achieving Success with GRACE
13. Authentic Leadership: Leading From Your Essence
14. Leveraging Your Networking for Career & Business Success
15. Stand Up & Speak Up
17. 4 Indispensable Strategies for Success
18. Thriving In a Down Economy
19. Evolve and Embrace Challenges As Opportunity for Growth
20. Dare to Be Different: Become an Enabler & Person of Value at Work
21. Attracting & Keeping Them: The Customers
22. Building and Leading Authentic Organisations
23. Creating a Delivery Focused Organisation: Transformation through Leadership
24. Enhancing Your Digital Leadership
25. Executive Presence: Gravitas, Grooming and Communications
26. Women and Breakthrough Leadership
27. Mastering Great Performance in Public Speaking
28. Building Personal Resilience in the Workplace
29. Women Empowerment: Becoming an authentic and inspirational leader of the 21stCentury
30. Time Management: Regaining Control over Time and Priorities
31. Strategic Leadership and Good Governance

If you will like to book Dayo Olomu for any of the above keynotes, programmes or you require executive coaching, please email: info@dayoolomu.com

Please note that Dayo also delivers 15 training courses in three main categories namely:
1. Management & Leadership Training
2. Customer Care Training
3. Personal Effectiveness training

Contact & Connect details:
Office: 0871 218 1773
Mob: + 44 7957 581 703 (UK)
Mob: + 234 803 973 6164 (Nigeria)
BB pin: 290A231D
Email: info@dayoolomu.com

My Purpose, Goal, Vision, Values, Philosophy & Legacy

My purpose in life is to use my creativity, skills, talents, knowledge, passions and enthusiasm to make a positive difference in the world, to serve God, transform lives and connect people to their destiny.

My statement of purpose: Through consulting, speaking, training, coaching, mentoring and writing, I desire to make a positive difference in the world, create momentum in people's lives by taking them from good to great and helping my clients to grow their people, performance and profits exponentially.

Mission statement: Be a thought leader in developing authentic, inspirational and transformational leaders who can translate vision into action with the help of others

My passion is adding value to lives, helping to grow people and helping organisations to increase productivity, performance and profit.

My core belief is that we are all endowed with the seeds of greatness.

My fulfilment is seeing the results of my principles and strategies being transformed into people's lives.

My core values, which underpin everything, I do revolve around 5Fs: Faith, Family, Fitness, Fairness and Friendship.

My FACE values which drives my business are: Fairness, Agility, Courage and Excellence.

My brand value is to offer value for money and quality products/services with fun and passion. I want my brand to incorporate innovation, cutting edge, class, style, panache, integrity, agility, tenacity, modernity and a can-do attitude. I want my intensity, anything-is-possible and pragmatic approach to inspire others.

My view of National Development is that to make our country great, we have a role to play starting with doing something in the community where we reside.

My motto is if you want to obtain something you've never had in your life you must be ready to do things you've never done before in your life.

My philosophy is to treat people not as I would like to be treated but to treat them as they wish to be treated according to their individual needs and to avoid making assumptions.

My professional mission is to inspire and empower people and organisations to reach higher levels of achievement and peak performance. "To motivate and inspire 1,000,000 people and/or organisations per year to higher levels of achievement and peak performance by providing information, tips, tools and strategies through speaking, seminar, writing, training, mentoring and coaching.

My personal mission is to give people a larger vision of themselves beyond their mental conditions and their current circumstances. To help people achieve their full potential. I want to be a catalyst of hope and an agent of positive change. We may not know what the future will bring, but we are responsible for what we bring to the future.

My new work in Africa is to help increase the level of human capital in the continent, increase the number of business leaders and entrepreneurs; develop effective communicators and public speakers; help people to conquer fear, to stop procrastination, to believe in themselves and to take action so that they can become the persons they are destined to be.

My areas of genius are speaking, training, coaching, consulting, writing, mentoring and TV presentations. I do these things easily and well and when I do them in a focus way, they are the things I get paid for the most.

My statement of promise as a speaker: This presentation is going to be my absolute best. It will be the finest expression of all I have within me to share. I will serve my client, spur positive action - and touch hearts. I will share my experience, bring out the best in my audience, and help them grow as they help themselves (or organisations) to grow. Through this surrender to my purpose I will earn referrals, new business and repeat business, too. These attitudes and actions validate my right to be known as an expert who speaks.

My first thought on stage: God let me speak the truth to these people and let my words impact them positively.

My ultimate goal is for all areas of my life to blossom like the tree tendered by the side of the river. Because the sum is greater than the parts.

My legacy is, when I get to the end of my life, I want to know that my life counted for something, that long after am gone, somehow my impact lives on. I want to know that I have done all that I could to make this world a better place, by positively enhancing the lives of those around me and helping thousands, if not millions, to become who they desired and achieve what they thought was impossible. I want to know that I gave everything my best shot. I maximised my potentials and stretched myself to the limit. Most importantly I serve God and that I am a good husband and father.

YOU GOT THE POWER to:

- Have Unshakable Believe In Yourself
- Set And Achieve Your Goals
- Move Beyond Positive Thinking To Positive Doing.
- Win By Keep Trying
- Take Your Business & Career To The Next Level
- Create Your Own Opportunity
- Conquer Fear
- Stop Procrastinating
- Turn Your Adversity To Success
- Associate With Positive People
- Design A Blueprint For Your Life
- Eliminate The Obstacles Blocking Your Path
- Be Successful
- Take Action Now!
- Create An Extra-ordinary Quality Of Life

17389976R00020

Printed in Great Britain
by Amazon